The Tale of Johnny Appleseed

A Story of Generosity

Retold by Christina Wilsdon
Illustrated by Jeff Fisher

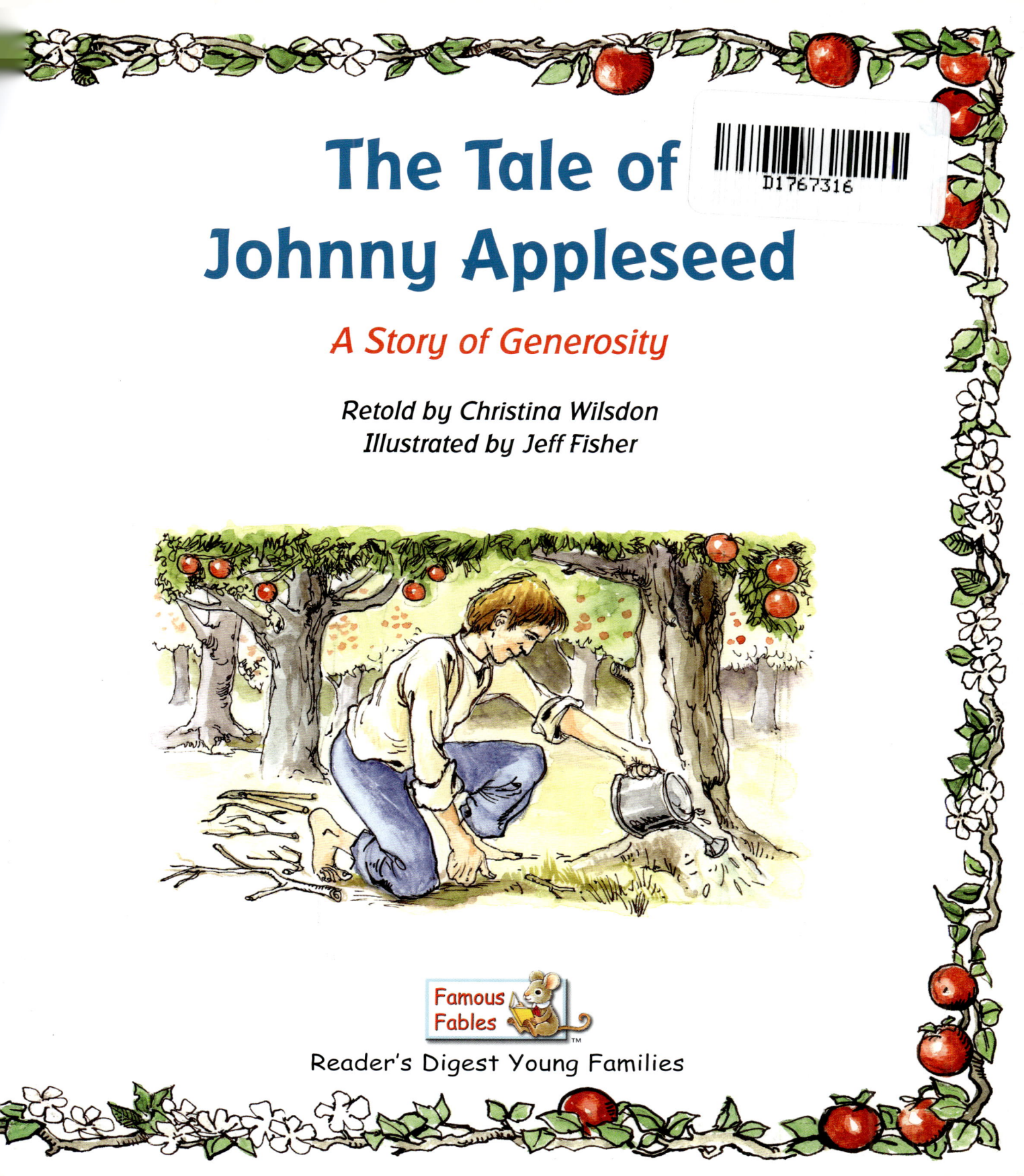

Famous Fables™

Reader's Digest Young Families

There once was a man named Johnny Appleseed. He lived on a little farm in Pennsylvania, where he kept a few goats and some chickens. Tidy rows of apple trees grew in his orchard. Bees buzzed among the trees. They lived in beehives that Johnny built for them. The bees filled the hives with sweet, golden honey.

Every now and then, Johnny took some of the honey, leaving the rest for the bees. He shared this honey with his neighbors. Whenever folks stopped by to say hello, he sent them home with a jar of it!

Johnny loved working in his orchard—pulling weeds, trimming branches, and watering the trees. Sometimes Johnny would stop work and sit in the orchard, listening to the birds sing and the bees buzz. He would lean against a tree's rough bark or perch in the branches. He liked to munch on an apple.

Johnny liked apple trees so much, he thought his neighbors would like them, too. He sold trees to those who wished to buy them. He gave them away to those who couldn't pay.

One night, Johnny dreamed of a land filled with sweet-smelling apple orchards. He dreamed of apple trees shading the ground in the American West, out on the frontier. When he woke up, he decided to make his dream come true.

"First I have to gather apple seeds," Johnny said to himself. So he visited all the apple-cider mills in the area. Cider mills crushed apples to make them into juice. The mill owners didn't need the seeds and were glad to give them to Johnny. Soon Johnny had many sacks filled with seeds.

The next day, Johnny gave his mule, his goats, his chickens, and his beehives to his neighbors. "Help yourselves to the apples on my trees," he told them.

Then he dug up a few of his tiniest new apple trees. Carefully, he packed their roots in dirt and tucked them into sacks. He loaded the young trees and sacks of seeds into two canoes that he tied together. Finally, he hopped into one of the canoes and paddled up the river. He waved to his neighbors lined up on the shore to say good-bye.

"Good luck, Johnny!" they shouted.

Johnny and his canoes went past fields and forests.
The rippling rivers carried him farther west each day.
Along the way, Johnny stopped to go ashore.

At every stop, Johnny slung a sack of apple seeds over his shoulder. Then he hiked across the fields and through the forests on bare feet, looking for any settlers living in the area. Sometimes, if the weather was dry, his feet stirred up clouds of dust. Sometimes, when it was wet or snowy, his feet churned up puddles of mud.

I've brought some apple seeds and seedlings for you," Johnny said to the settlers. "Plant them, keep them watered, and pull up the weeds. In a few years the seeds will grow into trees and will reward your hard work with a bumper crop of juicy apples."

"Thank you, Johnny," said the settlers. They gladly took some handfuls of seeds and a few seedlings. Then they repaid Johnny's generosity with their own.

"Won't you sit a spell and have some dinner with us?" they asked.

"Please stay!" cried the settlers' child.

"I'd be mighty pleased to join you," replied Johnny, "and thank you for your kindness."

Sometimes when Johnny hopped ashore, he did not find any settlers. But Johnny knew they would arrive someday.

"I'll just clear a patch in this woodland for an orchard," he said. He rubbed his hands together briskly. Then he grabbed the wooden handle of his ax.

Thwack! Thwack! Down came the trees. In their place, Johnny planted young apple trees. He smiled and thought how happy the new settlers would be to find apple trees waiting for them.

One winter day, Johnny met a farmer while walking through a town. He offered the man some apple seeds. The farmer, in return, gave Johnny a pair of warm shoes.

"Your poor bare feet could use these!" he said.

Johnny smiled. He'd been given shoes before, even though he preferred going barefoot. Just the same, he said, "Thank you very much."

The next day, Johnny and the farmer met each other again. The farmer was surprised to see Johnny's bare feet!

"What happened to the shoes I gave you?" he asked.

"I met a man who needed them more than I did," explained Johnny.

Johnny not only planted apple trees—he was also always ready to lend a hand. If people were lost in the forest and met Johnny, he always showed them the way. He freed animals from traps. He found lost, hungry ponies and took care of them. Then he gave them to grateful settlers in need of horses.

Although Johnny Appleseed lived a long time ago, some people think his generous spirit is still at work when they are helped by a kind stranger. And if a little apple tree springs up in a place where no one remembers planting a seed—why, that's a sign that maybe Johnny's still busy, doing what he loves best!

Famous Fables, Lasting Virtues Tips for Parents

Now that you've read The Tale of Johnny Appleseed, *use these pages as a guide to teach your child the virtues in the story. By talking about the story and its message and engaging in the suggested activities, you can help your child develop good judgment and a strong moral character.*

About Generosity

Children learn about generosity when they are encouraged to share toys at playtime and food at mealtimes. We also teach them about the spirit of generosity when we help them make or buy gifts for holidays and special occasions. Involving children in charitable activities—such as collecting money for causes or volunteering time and energy for projects—also teaches generosity. Here are a few ways to help children nurture their giving natures:

1. *Help others in your community.* Find age-appropriate activities to help others in which your child (and other family members) can become involved. Your place of worship, immediate neighborhood, community center, and animal shelters are all good places to look for activities that help others.

2. *Disaster relief.* Your child's school or other organization may sponsor fund-raising events or a collection of clothing, food, books, or household items to help people affected by a natural disaster, such as a hurricane or an earthquake. Talk with your child about the nature of the disaster and how he can help. (Any fund-raising should be adult-supervised, limited to people the child knows, and not involve door-to-door selling.)

3. *Gift-giving.* Giving gifts is a concrete way for children to learn about generosity. Making a gift not only engages a child's creativity, but also encourages him to focus on the recipient. Wrapping the gift and making a gift tag or card add a delightful bit of ceremony to further highlight the joy of giving.

4. *Allowance.* In some families, children are encouraged to divide their allowance into thirds—one-third for spending, one-third for saving, and one-third for charitable giving.